T0193693

HOLD THE LIGHT

HAIKU TO CONNECT WITH YOUR HIGHEST SELF

DONNA MICHELLE WREN

BALBOA.PRESS
A DIVISION OF HAY HOUSE

Balboa Press books may be ordered through booksellers or by contacting:

Balboa Press
A Division of Hay House
1663 Liberty Drive
Bloomington, IN 47403
www.balboapress.com
844-682-1282

Because of the dynamic nature of the Internet, any web addresses or
links contained in this book may have changed since publication and
may no longer be valid. The views expressed in this work are solely those
of the author and do not necessarily reflect the views of the publisher,
and the publisher hereby disclaims any responsibility for them.

The author of this book does not dispense medical advice or prescribe the use
of any technique as a form of treatment for physical, emotional, or medical
problems without the advice of a physician, either directly or indirectly. The
intent of the author is only to offer information of a general nature to help
you in your quest for emotional and spiritual well-being. In the event you use
any of the information in this book for yourself, which is your constitutional
right, the author and the publisher assume no responsibility for your actions.

Any people depicted in stock imagery provided by Getty Images are
models, and such images are being used for illustrative purposes only.
Certain stock imagery © Getty Images.

Print information available on the last page.

ISBN: 979-8-7652-2656-8 (sc)
ISBN: 979-8-7652-2655-1 (hc)
ISBN: 979-8-7652-2657-5 (e)

Library of Congress Control Number: 2022907861

Balboa Press rev. date: 04/22/2022

I dedicate this book to my daughters, Sarah & Julia. They are my greatest teachers and the two most beautiful lights of my life.

I dedicate this book to all beings, may we be peaceful, may we be happy, may we be safe. May we all awaken to the light of our true nature. May we all be free.

AUTHOR'S NOTE

This book was inspired by many aspects, spanning decades of my life. Back when I was a kid, my fifth-grade teacher, Mrs. Kinsberg, taught us haiku, and I was instantly enthralled. I love the precise, alternating 5, 7, 5 syllabic sentences and the sensual, beautiful, natural imagery that haiku paints upon a page. The beauty and self-discipline required to write haiku appeals to me in a deep and natural way. I am inspired by haiku's combination of precision and sensual beauty and while all my poems follow the 5 or 7 syllabic sentences, I do expand beyond the 3 sentence stanzas and sometimes play with the alternating syllabic sentences to allow for more creativity and flow.

Several years ago, I began writing posts for social media that were based on my own spiritual awakening. Later, I had the idea to gather all my posts and turn them into a book, but it didn't flow, it was missing something. And then one day in meditation, inspiration came to me – turn them into haiku. And that's when Hold the Light was born. The posts where the bija, the seed, of what I was growing and creating.

#11, the first haiku I wrote, became the title of this book. It wasn't until after I wrote this first haiku that I remembered back to when I first learned to meditate, that "I AM Light" was my very first mantra. My teacher asked us to choose our own mantra and so I chose "I AM Light" because I felt so lost in the darkness and heaviness of my life at that time. It took several years to break through fear, heartbreak, and uncertainty. I knew I had to leave one life and create a completely new one. I reconnected with my light and I protected it, nurtured it and fanned it into a bonfire. My lessons, innerstanding and the beauty all around us which helped to rekindle my light are all reflected in this book. It is my wish that the light that is infused in my haiku resonates in your heart and connects with your inner light.

I hope that my haiku reminds you, no matter where you are on your path, you always Hold the Light within you.

Sending love to all,

Donna Michelle

1

I am breathing in;

I am breathing out.

With every breath in,

I fill my body with light.

With every breath out,

I release the dark.

I breathe in the light;

I breathe out the dark.

I am lighter still

With every breath in

And every breath out.

2

Now in this moment,

Rise above the thunderstorm.

Chaos in your mind,

Meet your higher self

Peaceful, above the storm clouds.

She's always waiting

For you to remember you.

I am one with love.

3

Beautiful Gaia

Always holds her arms open.

Her emerald-green trees

Radiate love and healing.

Her waters cleanse us.

We're born breathing in her air;

We die giving back our breath.

She grounds our bare feet.

She nurtures, listens, and loves

Unconditionally, yes.

Reconnect with her,

Exalt and honor.

Remember, she is our queen.

4

Let go of the fish

To experience release.

Splash! You are both free.

5

There is more to the Universe

Than we'll ever know

In this human life.

And that is the point.

6

The mind gets caught up

In the labyrinth of thinking.

Close your eyes and breathe;

Feel your heart beat like a drum,

The sound bath of love.

Rise into the vibration

Of Source energy.

Now connect with your true self;

The answers will come.

Greater than thinking—just know.

7

What loving-kindness

Have you bestowed on yourself?

The others can wait.

Refill your own soul vessel,

And reach for the light

Stored up in your heart.

Forgive past choices.

Let go of all the old pain

That you tightly hold.

You're no longer that person

You see in the dark.

The why, the lessons, the growth—

You are awakened.

Now the light is always on,

So love on yourself.

Hold on to your inner child,

Kiss her soft forehead.

Tell her she is always safe;

You'll never leave her.

You can grow and bloom as one,

Fragments together.

8

Pink cherry blossoms

Open and share their perfume

For such a short time

Before they fall to the ground.

Your love is as sweet,

No matter how long it lasts.

9

With three eyes open,

It's not a coincidence;

It's orchestration.

The Universe's magic,

Always right on time.

10

First you plant the seeds

Then sit in liminal space,

Floating, uncertain.

Water, light, and hope,

Or dry, dark, and fear.

Choose how to feel in between.

It will make all the difference.

11

Hold the light, she says.

The dark is just too heavy.

12

The fears we don't face

Become our cages and walls,

So stare that fear down.

Kindly, tell it to fuck off.

13

Cheers! There is always

Some magic to celebrate!

The three of cups, *clink!*

14

The storm is coming.

It will rage all around you.

Will you brace against—

Soaking to the bone by rain,

Pummeled by sharp sleet,

Whipping wind against your face?

Or shelter within—

Find soft solace in your breath,

Feel your own heartbeat?

Every breath in and breath out,

The storm grows distant.

You find yourself in the eye,

Where the white crane flies.

15

At the end of class

The yogi says, "Namaste."

Such simple beauty

To honor the light within

Your heart and my heart,

From one soul to another.

16

When two swans make love,

Their necks become intertwined.

Two flames light as one

When the fire is sacred.

This love is divine,

Our own divinity

Expressing itself

In the highest vibration

With another soul.

17

The heart understands

How to see the light though faith

When the mind only

Sees darkness through fearful eyes.

18

Put your fear in the back seat.

Give it the iPad

So you can focus

On the road ahead.

19

Jumping into the circus?

You're one of the clowns

Walking upon the tightrope

Of judgment and fear.

Take off your clown mask.

Leave the big top; walk away

Into the night air,

Away from the spectacles.

Find your own dirt path

Into the quiet and peace

Of your own soul's voice.

20

Don't wait to receive

Flowers from anyone else.

Gift them to yourself.

21

Always remember

You alone are your shelter

From the iron rain,

Guilt, pelting down on your mind,

Violent winds of shame,

Desert of abandonment,

Dark isolation.

Your heart always beats with love.

Feel it through your hand,

Your own heart beating for you,

So loyal and true.

Hear what your heart has to say.

It always knows truth,

Never swayed by conditions

Outside of itself.

Go within and feel the love;

Even when it's quiet,

It will hold you in comfort

And give you the strength

To continue on your path

Toward the shining sun

Sparkling on the calming sea,

Through the depth and breadth

Of your ever-growing soul.

22

Once you awaken

Like the rising sun each day,

No matter the clouds,

Thunder, or rainstorm,

Your inner light shines

With your rising consciousness.

After the sun sets

In a dark sky filled with stars,

You light up the moon.

It is your own light

Illuminating the world.

23

Small white butterfly

Brings a message from Spirit

When you are awake.

24

You want love? Be love.

You want respect? Show respect.

You want joy? Be joy.

We cannot receive the light

We don't reflect out.

25

(My solar return haiku 2021)

Won't you dance with me

Beneath the stars and moonlight?

Silent, only for

Our beating hearts.

26

When it's uncertain

Is the most powerful time.

Connect with your heart.

Now choose how you want to feel.

This is your power.

27

Don't hate, meditate.

It's so much better for you.

Raise your vibration.

Imagine if we all did,

How the world would change.

We could lift the veil of fear,

Share the love within,

Embrace our differences.

The core is the same—

To be happy and peaceful,

To be free to choose

What makes your heart sing and dance,

To be loved and seen

For your true authentic self.

Take a deep breath in.

Slowly release the exhale,

And focus your mind

Just on one breath at a time.

I will meet you there.

28

Creation through love
Is the highest vibration.

29

As the moon dances

Her way closer to the sun,

Their energy builds

Until they are face-to-face

Celestial lovers,

Both giving and receiving

To one another

Fire and luminescence

Just for a short time,

Embracing one another.

Their light and darkness

Mirroring one another

Until they move on

Through the sky into longing

Until the next time

Fate aligns them in oneness.

30

Faith is seeing light

With deep knowing in your heart,

When all your eyes see

Is the abyss of darkness.

31

What if you were to

Expect the unexpected

And it's wonderful?

32

At the end of day,

Setting down your empty bowl,

You see it is filled

With all your flowing desires

Not yet realized.

The emptiness is so rich

As a guide down your next path,

He will gladly die

As a martyr for your growth

As you fill your bowl,

Instead, with each desire

Brought to fruition.

33

"Watering the roots,"

Tiny needles guide the flow.

Unblock energy!

34

Sitting in the sun,

An orchestra of birdsong

Fills my heart and soul.

35

Tender new buds,

Pure potentiality.

36

Musea, my muse,

My spark of inspiration.

When she visits me,

My mind and heart become one.

37

When you're a desert,

A drop of water will do.

Be an oasis,

And you are the waterfall,

Discernment flowing.

You choose who swims in your pool.

38

Goddess Moon reflects

Back to us our phases

Mirror in the sky.

New moon, black in the nightscape,

Hiding in plain sight.

In her darkness, she begins:

Blank slate—new cycle

Before the light, Genesis.

Create in darkness.

As she becomes the crescent,

Set your intentions.

Gather your thoughts and make plans.

All will grow with her.

In her first quarter,

Slow momentum grows.

Inspired action!

Baby steps in alignment

With your soul's calling.

As a gibbous queen,

She invokes intensity,

Anticipation!

So close to the main event,

All our senses

Heightened to see, taste, and touch

All we desire.

Empress of fullness,

High priestess of all knowing,

A shining beacon

To gather, harvest, seeds sown,

All that you toiled.

All that did not grow.

Culmination and release.

Bask in her full light

For it's your own reflection

Of all you create.

Exhale gratitude.

The bright queen removes her crown.

Wanes to turn inward,

Still beaming with joy.

In her third quarter,

She is ready to let go,

Thankful for lessons.

Time to cut cords that bind her.

Break away, be free.

Now just a sliver,

She surrenders to darkness.

Recuperate, rest,

Feel her emptiness

Just before she disappears

To begin again.

39

Upon waking up

We begin to remember

We are connected

To everything—seen, unseen.

Separateness, a lie,

An illusion we were taught.

Divided we fall;

Together we rise, in love.

40

We cry, the water.

We burn with passion, the fire.

We breathe life, the air.

We grow from a seed, the earth.

Let water cleanse you.

Let fire ignite your heart.

Let air carry you.

Let the earth ground all your fears.

Flowing with water,

Rising in the flame of fire,

Soaring on the air,

Standing in strength on the earth.

Connect, listen, know.

Remember: you are Spirit

Embodied in all—

Water, fire, air, and earth.

Consciousness alive,

Expressing itself through us.

41

My soul's song sings out;

I am becoming more me.

Beauty unfolding,

Letting go of all the weight,

Binding, and boxes

That keep me small and managed.

The light hurts my eyes,

But I will never go back.

My sight will adjust,

And I will follow the light

Of my own soul song.

I am becoming more me,

And she's feeling free.

Thank you, Dave Matthews, my muse #41.

42

To light one candle

With the flame from another,

This is our purpose.

43

Washing the dishes

Thankful for running water.

Turned to a trickle,

Cleansing the plate and my mind.

Rainbow bubbles, *pop!*

44

As I hold the broom,

Settling into rhythm,

Sweeping dirt away,

Clean slate to begin the day,

My path becomes clear.

45

The deepest knowing,

Unwavering truth,

Is always felt in your gut.

Do not ever doubt

What you feel in your body.

It will never lie.

46

Fire signs ablaze,

Burning bright with energy.

Highest expressions—

Passion, confidence, power,

Optimistic, creative,

Independent, ambitious.

Loyal, free spirits

Rise like the flames in your heart,

Phoenix from the ash

Be yourself, Aries.

Let your mane down; roar, Leo.

Be free and roam, Sag.

Earth signs ground us all,

Creating reality.

Touch, taste, hear, see, smell

From the ether into form.

Highest expressions—

Persistent, responsible,

Driven, determined,

Sensual, healing, loving.

Majestic mountains

Deeply rooted in the earth.

Be strong, beautiful Taurus.

You're perfect, Virgo.

You deserve rest, Capricorn.

Air signs bring the change

Beginning with our thoughts.

First comes the idea,

Inspiration and magic

The eyes cannot see

But real, nonetheless.

Highest expressions—

Freedom, fairness, righteousness.

Communication,

Curious, chatty, witty,

Fun-loving, romantic,

Innovative, sociable,

Individualistic.

Banter and wit, Gemini.

Sweep me off my feet, Libra.

Change the world, Aquarius.

Water signs feel all the feels.

Emotions run deep.

Quench our thirst for connection.

To know you're alive

Is to feel it all.

Highest expressions—

Intuitive, deep,

Insightful, empathetic,

Nurturing, dreamy,

Sexy, imaginative,

Protective, faithful.

You are your own home, Cancer.

Scorpios always know truth.

Sail away with me, Pisces.

None of us are just one sign.

We are the whole wheel.

Embrace all the elements,

Become your best self.

47

Each human body,

Divinely aligned within,

Seven energies

Flowing from our root to crown.

When we are balanced,

The soul and body are one.

Chakras, spinning wheels

Energy in alignment.

Start each day anew.

Close your eyes, breathe deep, and see

Each chakra ablaze,

Each color in the rainbow,

Pure energy light.

Affirm out loud to yourself:

"I *am* rooted, safe.

I *am* creative, sexy.

I *am* confident.

I *am* love, compassionate.

I *am* expressive.

I *am* intuitive, sure.

I *am* one with all.

Your power lies within you.

Come back home again

As many times as you need.

The door is always open.

48

Up on steep, high hills,

Unwavering lighthouse stands.

Elements weathered,

Solitary, unchanging.

Seasons come and go.

Years pass, clouds of black and blue,

A fortress of light,

A faithful beacon guiding

In the darkest night

As moon rests from reflection.

Never chasing ships,

Simply hold the light within.

49

Unpack your heavy

Bags filled with conditioning,

Family, society,

Cultural, political,

Religious, educational.

Empty, release each layer.

Unlearn everything,

Unearth authenticity.

This is your purpose.

Carry only light,

And to your own self be true.

50

Even the most tattered quilt

Has a silver lining.

51

As the butterfly

Emerges out of darkness,

She flies right away.

She's beautiful right away.

We admire her new form.

Do we acknowledge

The darkness and pain,

Complete destruction of self,

Harsh isolation?

Certainty in her purpose,

Caterpillar consumes all

Only for her growth.

But vital to her purpose,

She must be selfish

To achieve cocoon.

It is in the becoming,

All the necessary steps,

Solitary path,

So she can emerge

Not just for beauty

That is a means to the end.

Beauty is her protection,

So she can fulfill her purpose,

A pollinator.

Now, as she sustains herself,

She sustains us all.

52

What if all the pain—

Searing, subtle, violent pain,

Heartbreaking loss, lies,

Abandonment, rejection,

Cruelty, exclusion,

Judgmental knives to your heart,

Ice-cold erasure,

Stripping, stealing innocence,

Crippling loneliness—

What if all this pain

In all its forms has purpose?

One single purpose—

The call to heal ourselves through love.

A deep, desperate call,

A howling, guttural call,

A soft whispering,

A tearful begging,

Our soul's call to rise up

From our dark graves

Buried beneath all this pain,

Unearthing our heart.

Holding our inner child

In safety and care,

In softness and tenderness,

In understanding,

In kindness and compassion,

Holding his or her small hand

Gently in your hand,

Sending healing energy

To old wounds, heartbreak,

Releasing painful patterns.

Filling in with love

All the places that still hurt,

Building up new trust,

Never again abandon

Your innocent self,

Always loving yourself more,

Following your bliss,

Living free, authentically,

Manifesting your dreams,

Staying true to all of you.

This is how we heal,

Answering the call with love

Again and again,

As many times as it takes

Until you are whole.

53

Holding the light within you

Is as vital as

Breathing the air within you,

Drinking clean water,

Sleeping peacefully at night,

Sharing joy with friends,

Feeling loved and safe and seen.

Never losing hope

Even in the darkest times.

Holding the light within you

May light a new path

Toward a way we never knew.

When all else has failed—

Fallen away, broken down—

Hold the light within,

And all can never be lost.

Hold the light within,

And a bright, new day will dawn

54

Change is all there is.

The tides are always rolling.

The clouds never still,

The grass is always growing,

The sun and moon dance

Across the sky, day and night.

And yet we forget,

Despite our intelligence,

That nothing will last,

And still we become attached

To all that must end

In one way or another.

All in Samsara.

The suffering we create

Is the only way

We humans can ever learn

Through loss, pain, and grief.

I believe this is the truth

Of our human life.

Polarity is the way

To teach appreciation

For there is no grief

Without first feeling deep love,

And so it must be,

Like leaves falling from the trees,

We learn to let go.

All will bloom again in Spring.

55

Calling all healers—

Upon waking every day,

Reignite your light.

Vibrate with kindness,

Compassion, love, joy, and truth.

But never forget,

Conjure your boundary bubble

Like Glinda the Good

Before dealing with muggles.

56

When your world is uncertain

But you learn to walk

By faith and not with your eyes,

Releasing your grip

On the old, fallen tree trunk,

Half-submerged and yet

Clinging to the riverbank.

Only then can you enter

Into the current

Flowing with the Universe

Without pain, struggle.

Floating on your back with ease,

Sunshine on your face,

You'll arrive in divine time

Upon your next path.

57

All is vibration

Within all matter, all form,

All that we can see,

And all that we cannot see.

Every thought, feeling,

Every tree upon the Earth,

Soft, Summer breezes,

Lips kissing, soft, warm embrace,

Silent snow falling,

Every blossoming flower,

A baby's first cry.

Hurtful words, icy-cold gaze,

Earth quaking apart,

Final goodbye to your love,

Fierce hurricane gales,

Jaw-dropping devastation

At the hands of men

Shooting guns or chopping trees.

Every vibration

Ripples like a stone

Thrown into a silent lake.

Understand this truth,

Awaken to your power,

Use it wisely and with love.

58

Forgiveness lets go,

Unravelling the tight knot.

Your heart, untethered,

Once anchored by pain's lead weight

To soar free again.

59

Winter's voice whispers,

Shhh, as nature settles down.

Cold winds, frozen ground,

Bare branches, no running sap.

Snow falls silently.

If I listen to her call,

Flow with her rhythm,

My strong beating heart will slow,

My quick breath deepen.

Into the cave of my mind,

Sitting by the lake,

A mirror of my soul's self,

Quiet reflection.

My choices create my path,

Footprints in the snow

I forge as I go,

Trusting my own inner voice.

She guides me beyond.

Settle down; just be present.

Lay in the clearing

Beneath a great evergreen.

Blanket of fresh snow,

Rest, her offering.

Sacred stillness, silence heard.

Winter's voice whispers

Her own sweet lullaby.

60

Spring's great stretch, slow yawn.

Soft kisses on my forehead,

Warm breath on my skin,

Gently awakens my heart

To more light each day.

Cleansing rain washes away

Remnants, snowy sleep.

Feathered harbinger arrives,

Red-breasted robin

Upon the budding branches.

61

Dog days of Summer

Lying in the sun, panting.

Water the garden

Before the midday wilting.

Everything is green,

Earth's heart chakra in full bloom.

Bees and butterflies

Pollinate, sustain us all.

Intoxicating

Lilac perfume sends me back,

My youth, summer love

Practicing patience each day.

My mouth salivates

For the ripened Jersey Girl.

Eat the tomato

Like an apple, juicy, sweet,

Dripping down my chin.

62

Autumn bittersweet,

More like salted caramel.

Reap what we have sown.

Sleep with the windows open.

Night crickets' last set.

Cooler air brings peaceful dreams.

Trees take center stage,

Their decay, so beautiful,

Like my singing bowl.

Each new day the palette adds

Glowing, vibrant hues,

Sunsets falling from branches.

Printed in the United States
by Baker & Taylor Publisher Services